NOTE BY THE COMPOSER

Hiyoku was written for the clarinetists Ayako and Charlie Neidich, whose performances were so out-standing that I chose to write this piece in the fall of 2001 for them. I asked Ayako to suggest a title and she explained it: "a very special poetic word originally used by the ancient Chinese poet, Bai Juyi, and adopted by old Japanese authors, meaning two birds flying together with the connotation of eternal love."

> ". . . *In the heavens we shall be two wings*
> *Flying side by side.*
> *On earth two roots*
> *Intertwined into one stem! . . .*"

—Elliott Carter

ANMERKUNG DES COMPONISTEN

Hiyoku ist den Klarinettisten Ayako und Charles Neidich gewidmet, deren Spiel so herausragend ist, dass ich mich im Herbst 2001 dazu entschloss, dieses Stück zu schreiben. Ich bat Ayako, den Titel vorzuschlagen, und sie erklärte ihn so: "ein ganz besonderes poetisches Wort, das ursprünglich von dem alten chinesischen Diethter Bai Juyi gebraught und dann von alten japanischen Autoren adaptiert wurde. Es bezeichnet den gemeinsamen Flug zweier Vögel und is konnotiert mit ewiger Liebe. „

> ". . . *Im Himmel werden wir zwei Flügel sein,*
> *Seite an Seite fliegend,*
> *auf Erden zwei Wurzeln*
> *sich windend zu einem Stamm . . .* „

—Elliott Carter

NOTE DU COMPOSITEUR

Hiyoku a été composé pour les clarinettistes Ayako et Charles Neidich, dont les préstations sont si extraordinaires que j'ai choisi d'écrire cette pièce pour eux en automne 2001. J'ai demandé a Ayako de suggerer un titre, et elle l'a expliqué de cette façon : « hikoyu, un mot particulièrement poétique utilisé à l'origine par l'ancien poète chinois Bai Juyi et adopté par les anciens poètes Japonais qui sig-nifie : deux oiseaux volant ensemble avec la connotation de l'amour éternel. »

> « . . . *Dans le ciel nous serions deux ailes*
> *volant côte à côte.*
> *Sur la terre deux racines*
> *s'embrassant pour être une tige! . . .* »

—Elliott Carter

CHAMBER MUSIC OF
ELLIOTT CARTER

TRIPLE DUO (1983)   20'
for flute (doubling piccolo), clarinet (doubling Eb and
bass clarinets), percussion, piano, violin, and cello

CHANGES (1983)   7'
for guitar

CANON FOR 4 (1984)   4'
"Homage to William"
for flute, bass clarinet, violin and cello

RICONOSCENZA PER GOFFREDO
   PETRASSI (1984)   4'
for solo violin

ESPRIT RUDE / ESPRIT DOUX (1984)   4'
pour Pierre Boulez
for flute and Bb clarinet

STRING QUARTET NO. 4 (1986)   24'

ENCHANTED PRELUDES (1988)   6'
for flute and cello

BIRTHDAY FLOURISH (1988)   1'
for five trumpets or brass quintet

CON LEGGEREZZA PENSOSA (1990)   5'
Omaggio a Italo Calvino
for Bb clarinet, violin, and cello

SCRIVO IN VENTO (1991)   5'
for solo flute

QUINTET (1991)   20'
for piano and winds

TRILOGY (1992)   17'
   Bariolage *for solo harp*   7'
   Inner Song *for solo oboe*   5'
   Immer Neu *for oboe and harp*   5'

GRA (1993)   4'
for solo Bb clarinet

GRA (1993)   4'
transcribed for trombone by Benny Sluchin

TWO FIGMENTS
for solo cello
   No. 1 (1994)   5'
   No. 2 – Remembering Mr. Ives (2001)   3'

TWO FRAGMENTS
for string quartet
   No. 1 – in memoriam David Huntley (1994)   4'
   No. 2 (1999)   3'

ESPRIT RUDE / ESPRIT DOUX II (1994)   5'
for flute, clarinet and marimba

OF CHALLENGE AND OF LOVE (1995)   25'
five poems of John Hollander
for soprano and piano

STRING QUARTET NO. 5 (1995)   20'

A 6 LETTER LETTER (1996)   3'
for solo English horn

QUINTET (1997)   10'
for piano and string quartet

LUIMEN (1997)   12'
for trumpet, trombone, mandolin, guitar, harp,
and vibraphone

SHARD (1997)   3'
for solo guitar

TEMPO E TEMPI (1998)   15'
for soprano, violin, English horn, and bass clarinet

FRAGMENT NO. 2 (1999)   3'
for string quartet

TWO DIVERSIONS (1999)   8'
for solo piano

RETROUVAILLES (2000)   3'
for solo piano

4 LAUDS (1984-2000)   11'
for solo violin
   Statement – Remembering Aaron (1999)   3'
   Riconoscenza per Goffredo Petrassi (1984)   4'
   Rhapsodic Musings (2000)   2'
   Fantasy – Remembering Roger (1999)   3'

OBOE QUARTET (2001)   17'
for oboe, violin, viola, and cello

HIYOKU (2001)   4'
for two clarinets

STEEP STEPS (2001)   3'
for bass clarinet

AU QUAI (2002)   3'
for bassoon and viola

RETRACING (2002)   3'
for solo bassoon

CALL (2003)   1'
for two trumpets and horn

INTERMITTENCES (2005)   6'
for solo piano

HENDON MUSIC

BOOSEY & HAWKES

U.S. $9.95

ISBN-13: 978-1-4234-1035-5

Distributed By

HAL LEONARD

48019132   9 781423 410355

DISTRIBUTED BY
HAL•LEONARD®
CORPORATION
7777 W. BLUEMOUND RD. P.O. BOX 13819 MILWAUKEE, WI 53213

ISMN M-051-19438-3

3

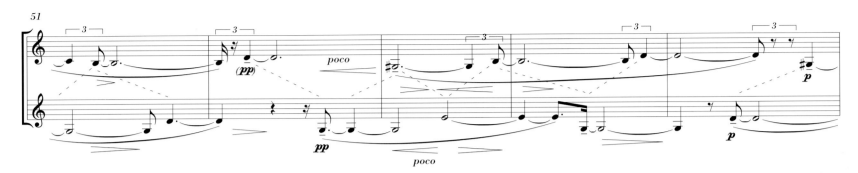

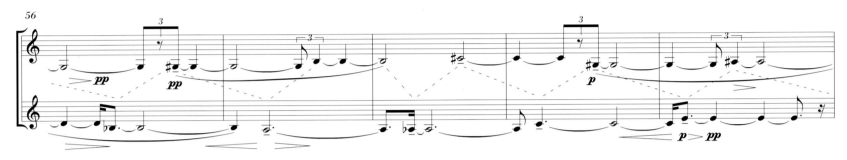

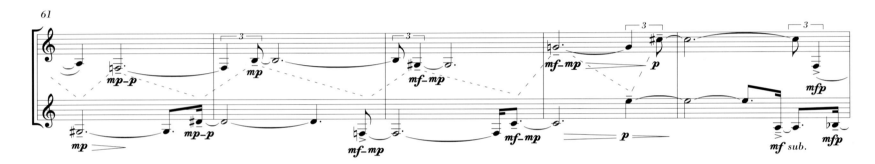

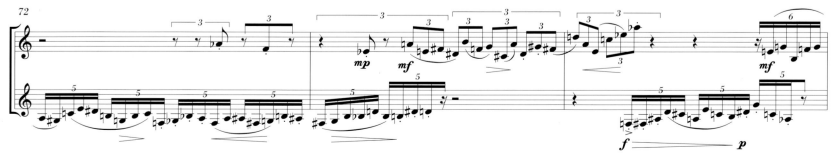

ELLIOTT CARTER

HIYOKU

比翼

for two clarinets

HENDON MUSIC

BOOSEY & HAWKES

DISTRIBUTED BY
Hal • Leonard®

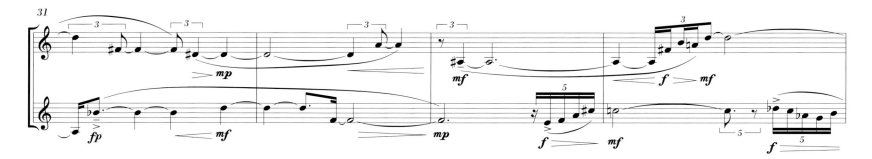

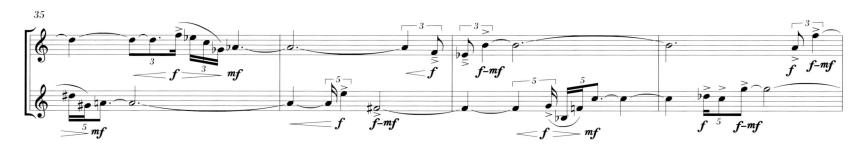

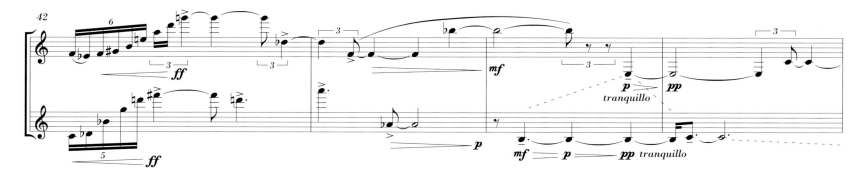

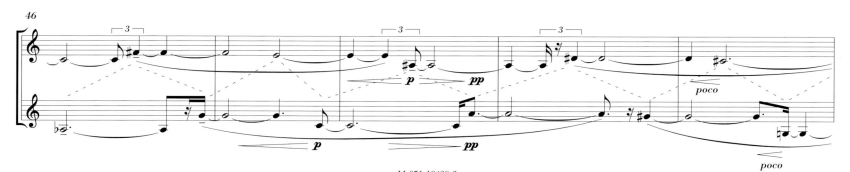

for Ayako and Charles Neidich

HIYOKU

Elliott Carter
(2001)

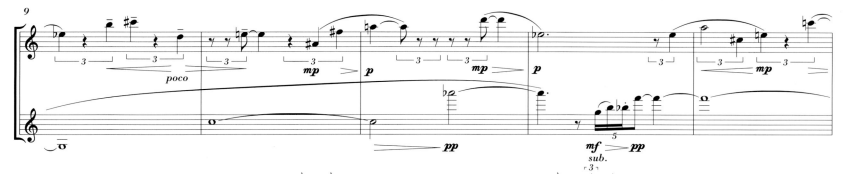

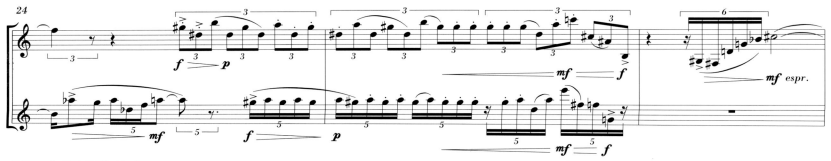

M-051-10438-3

Printed in U.S.A.

First performed December 9, 2001 at Kleine Zaal, Concertgebouw, Amsterdam
by Charles Neidich and Ayako Oshima, clarinets

First recorded by Charles Neidich and Ayako Oshima, clarinets,
on Bridge Records 9128

Duration: 4 minutes

Shuji artist (cover image): Teruhiro Takahashi